Paddlesteamers
and Riverboats
River Murray of the
By Peter Christopher

Cover photo: **PS Marion**.
Rear cover **PB Proud Mary**.

AXIOM

Other books by the Author.

South Australian Shipwrecks.
A Data Base. 1802-1989.
"To save the lives of strangers".
(Famous Shipwrecks of South Australia).
Shores of Tragedy.
(Shipwrecks of South Australia).
Divers' Guide to South Australia

All modern photos in this book have been taken by the author unless otherwise acknowledged.

ISBN: 978 18647604 0 8

CONTENTS

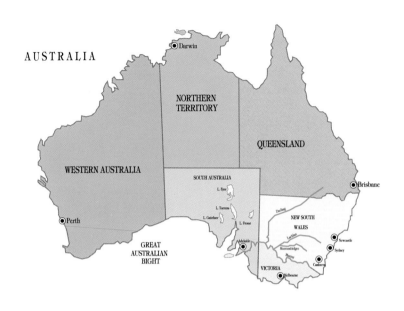

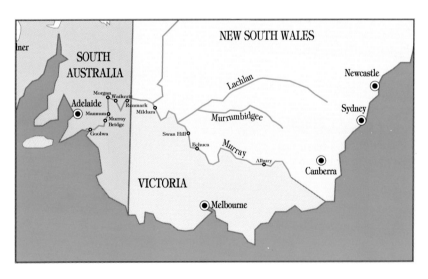

PREFACE

The River Murray is one of the most magnificent parts of Australia. Its still waters, its towering cliffs, forests, lagoons and a large variety of bird life are a delight to see.

The River supports over 350 varieties of birds, together with many species of mammals, reptiles and fish.

The world's largest redgum forest at Barmah depends upon its waters for survival.

The Murray, Darling, Lachlan and Murrumbidgee Rivers network has a combined length of 6,500 kilometres. Although locks and weirs now control the river flow they allow the passage of vessels along most of its length.

Stretching over 2500 kilometres from its source in the Mt. Kosciusko high country to where it flows into the Great Southern Ocean at Goolwa the Murray was the commercial highway for the working paddlesteamers which travelled upon it.

The romantic era of working paddlesteamers may have passed, but evidence of that time remains.

Today we no longer see hundreds of these vessels upon the river, but sufficient remain on or near the Murray for us to have a glimpse of what it must have been like so many years ago.

Today's riverboats are a mixture of original vessels that have been painstakingly restored and modern boats, many of which have been modelled upon the original paddlesteamers. Several of the newer boats are steam driven, with wood fired engines. Diesel engines not only power some new boats, but have been used in some restored 'old timers'.

This book presents photos and information about those historic paddlesteamers which you can still see today, whether working, on display or laid up, as well as several more modern vessels. It is not intended to be a substantial history, but rather a helpful guide to most of the significant boats on the River Murray today.

Interesting facts about life upon the Murray are included as 'River Tales' throughout the book.

The Murray River was once a major shipping highway, with hundreds of thousands of tons of cargo and produce being moved annually between South Australia, Victoria, New South Wales and Queensland.

Cargo into and out of Australia also entered and left by way of ports at Melbourne and those linked to Goolwa in South Australia. The 1850's saw a demand for riverboats to quickly and cheaply move large stocks of grain, wool and other produce to and from major river settlements.

In 1851 Port Elliot was designated as the outlet for the River Murray trade. The South Australian Governor, Sir Henry Young, had developed a plan for the River Murray trade to be brought to Goolwa by boat and linked to Port Elliot by a railway. Ships would load or unload cargo at Port Elliot as the closest sea port to the river port of Goolwa.

In 1853 the **PS Mary Ann** was the first paddlesteamer to be launched in the Murray, at Mannum, where its boiler is on display today. Twenty years later there were 240 boats operating on the River.

The demand for working riverboats continued until the turn of the century, when modern rail and road transport took over their role. At this time many vessels fell into disrepair and were abandoned or broken up. Fortunately, many have survived and been restored to their former glory.

Vessels are not fixed structures, and move frequently, sometimes hundreds of kilometres. Today, as in the past, they move to where their owners can obtain work. It is not uncommon for vessels shown to be in a particular location to be found elsewhere.

A number of vessels are currently being built or undergoing restoration and I hope to include these in future editions. In addition to the boats contained in this book, there are also a growing number of smaller, privately owned vessels upon the River.

The new role for paddle boats as leisure craft may yet enable their numbers to grow.

Although imperial measurements are the recognised standard for boats, I have used metric in this book, as many people are now unfamiliar with the former.

Throughout this book the initials PS refer to Paddlesteamer, PB to Paddle Boat where it is not steam driven, and MV to Motor Vessel for boats without paddles.

Thank you to all who have helped in the production of this book. Owners, volunteers, boat builders and crews have, without exception, provided every assistance.

RIVER TALES

The Early Explorers

Following colonisation of Australia's east coast, the Blue Mountains presented an obstacle to expansion westwards.

It was only after the crossing of the mountain barrier in 1813 that exploration started westwards and exploration of the river system began.

Initial surveys did not focus on the River Murray but instead upon the Lachlan, Darling and Murrumbidgee Rivers.

In 1817 John Oxley found two major rivers flowing westwards and believed that they flowed into an inland sea.

It was 1830 before Captain Charles Sturt explored the Murrumbidgee River and followed it into the Murray. His exploration along the entire length of the Murray established that its mouth was in the vicinity of Goolwa in South Australia.

Sir Thomas Mitchell in 1836 continued the exploration of these rivers, with many people still believing that an inland sea existed.

These three explorers played a vital role in opening up the South East of Australia. After Sturt and Mitchell squatters quickly followed and established communities along the River.

GOOLWA

Goolwa represents the end of the line for the River Murray, the point at which the river meets the sea. The mouth of the Murray today, however, is now a small gap between the sand hills, a direct result of the numerous locks and weirs which control the water flow along its length.

In its heyday Goolwa was a thriving river port which catered not only for riverboats but also for boats entering the river system from the ocean in the days when the mouth of the Murray was wide enough and deep enough to allow such passage. The Goolwa wharf, built in 1852 saw the town thrive for the next 40 years, making it one of Australia's major river ports. Sixty vessels were built at Goolwa up to 1913 including 37 paddlesteamers.

In a 1854 the first public railway in Australia was built running from Goolwa to Port Elliot. At the time Port Elliot was established as a port of some significance, although it soon proved to be totally unsuitable with several ships wrecked within its bay.

The 'Father of the modern day Riverboat', Captain Keith Veenstra set up a business building riverboats at Goolwa, with the first Aroona, built in the 1960s and followed by the current **Aroona, River Murray Queen, Murray Princess** and the Paddle Boat **Goolwa**.

The building of railway links to Morgan in 1878 and Murray Bridge in 1886 had a major impact on the river trade to Goolwa, as cargo was sent directly to Adelaide from these centres.

Like many river towns, Goolwa is today a tourist destination with a number of boats operating from its historic wharf.

PS Oscar W

Built at Echuca in 1908 the Oscar W spent the initial part of her working life carrying freight along the Murrumbidgee, Edward and Wakool rivers. The owner/builder, Charlie Wallin, named the vessel after his son, Oscar.

Sold in 1914 to Permewan, Wright and Company the **Oscar W** spent the next five years carrying wool in the Riverina region. The **Oscar W** was again sold in 1919 and continued to carry wool as well as general cargo on the Darling River.

In 1942 the vessel was purchased by George Ritchie of Goolwa but he quickly resold her as wartime restrictions made it difficult to refit the vessel. The new owner was equally unable to refit her as a tourist vessel and in 1943 the **Oscar W** was purchased by the South Australian Highways and Local Government Department where she was used for ferry maintenance while based at Morgan.

The **Oscar W** was again sold and in 1960 was moved to Mildura and used for tourist trips. After a short period of time at Echuca the **Oscar W** was again sold and moved back to South Australia. In 1985 the vessel was purchased by the South Australian Department of Tourism. Restoration work commenced in 1987 at Murray Bridge and in 1988 the **Oscar W** made her own way down to Goolwa where she was recommissioned on the first of July by the Minister of Tourism.

The **Oscar W** is owned by the South Australian Government but is on lease to the District Council where she is the flagship of Signal Point, the River Murray Interpretive Centre at Goolwa.

The **Oscar W** is maintained and operated by the 'Friends of the **Oscar W**', a dedicated group of volunteers.

PS Oscar W

Dimensions	31.5m x 6.3m x 1.6m, Composite
Built	1908, Echuca
Paddle wheel locations	Side
Engine	2 cylinder, 16 HP, wood burning steam engine. The engine was converted from wood to oil burning between 1945 to 1964 .

The **Oscar W** holds the record for the largest load of wool carried from the River Darling. Between 1943 and 1959 the Oscar W was used for ferry maintenance from a base at Morgan.

In 1962 the **Oscar W** towed the **PS Gem** to Swan Hill where it was to be part of the Pioneer Settlement complex. Six months of the trip was spent stranded by low River levels.

The original builder and owner was Charlie Wallin, who named the vessel after his son, Oscar.

MV Progress

Dimensions   12.2m x 3.4m x 1.0m, Wood

Built   1924, Port Adelaide

Engine   6 Cyl. Morris petrol

The **Progress** was one of the SA Farmers Union fleet of milk boats that operated collecting milk from surrounding dairies for the factory at Murray Bridge.

Progress is moored at Goolwa and is used as a private pleasure boat. The only other surviving milk boat of the fleet still in use on the water is the **Loyalty**, which conducts tours out of Wentworth. Another of the fleet, the **Union** is being restored at Murray Bridge.

Federal

Dimensions   21.6m x 4.3m x 1.1m, composite

Built   1902, Morgan

Paddle wheel locations   Side

Federal was owned by SA Government for 25 years from 1928.

In 1953 the **Federal** was converted to a houseboat, and for some years was known as **Ipana**. It is now a Bed & Breakfast, permanently attached to the river bed, after being totally refurbished in 1996.

Federal overlooks the Goolwa barrages, surrounded permanently by magnificent water birds.

Goolwa

Dimensions	33.5m x 8m x 0.75m, Steel
Built	1982 Goolwa
Paddle wheel location	Stern
Engine	Diesel

Goolwa is a modern mobile private houseboat for live aboard owners, and also a Bed and Breakfast at its Goolwa wharf moorings.

The **Goolwa** is a 3/4 scale model of the Sternwheeler **Captain Sturt** which was built in 1915 and disassembled in 1998. The wheel of the **Captain Sturt** has been used on the **Goolwa**.

PS William Randell

Dimensions   18.9m x 4.3m x 0.5m

Built   1998 Goolwa

Paddle wheel locations   Side

Engine   1923 7 HP wood fired steam

The vessel has been constructed in the traditional method by its owner, Roley Bartlett, and named after Captain William Randell who launched Australia's first Paddlesteamer, **Mary Ann**, at Mannum in 1853.

Moored on Hindmarsh Island overlooking the Goolwa wharf, **William Randell** is in all respects a magnificent reproduction of the boats of a century ago.

MV Aroona

Dimensions	28m x 6m x 0.9m
Built	1980, Goolwa

The **Aroona** is a modern tourist vessel with capacity to carry up to 140 passengers.

It was purpose built so that the vessel fits through the lock at Goolwa to allow access to the Murray mouth and the Coorong beyond. A unique feature of **Aroona** cruises is the change from fresh water to salt as the vessel moves though the lock in the Goolwa barrage.

The first **Aroona** was a 13.1m timber motor vessel built in 1966 at Goolwa. It was renamed the **Berribee Lee** about 1978 after it was sold.

Murray River Queen

Dimensions	50m x 14m x 1m
Built	Goolwa, 1973
Paddle wheel locations	Side
Engine	Diesel

The '**Queen**' was for many years a popular cruise boat on the Murray, but lay unused at Mannum for 3 years before being moved back to Goolwa. It was the first of the large Murray cruise vessels built by Captain Keith Veenstra.

The '**Queen**' is now a floating motel at the Goolwa wharf.

Tug Leo

Dimensions   17.4m x 3.2m x 1.2m

Built   1882, Sydney

Engine   Original steam converted to diesel

Leo was restored 1991-98, and is now the floating home of the owners of the Goolwa Maritime Gallery.

Leo was used as a cane tug to tow 6 to 8 barges. It was found on an arm of the Richmond River in northern NSW, and restored by its current owners.

The **Leo** forms part of the tourist complex of the Goolwa Maritime Gallery together with the Chart Room and Hector's Shed, which house River artefacts, pictures and chandlery.

18

RIVER TALES

The First Riverboats

The first riverboats moved quietly along the water, barely causing a ripple or disturbing the nearby birds and wildlife.

For many thousands of years before white settlement of Australia the Aborigines lived in harmony with their environment, with large numbers living along the entire length of the River Murray. It was an ideal environment with ready access to food and water.

Aboriginal canoes were constructed by cutting the bark off huge redgums and shaping and packing the ends to make them watertight. Shaping of the already curved bark was finished by softening it over fire, and by the use of fibre ropes to bring the sides together.

The canoes were capable of carrying two to three people, although stability was obviously affected by any more than one person.

Today it is possible to see some of these huge trees near the River with a section of their bark having been removed for the making of canoes. The removal of bark only took place on one side of the tree enabling it to continue to live and grow.

Proud Mary

Dimensions	33.4m x 9.75m x 1.0m
Built	Berri, 1981
Paddle wheel location	Stern
Engine	2 x Hino EH700 Diesel

The **Proud Mary** looks like a stern wheeler, but is driven by screw propellers off diesel engines. The decorative stern wheel is turned by the flow of water.

Proud Mary undertakes cruises of up to five nights on the lower Murray up to Blanchetown.

Captain Proud

Dimensions   24.6m x 9.1m x 1.0m

Built   1977, Pt. Adelaide

Paddle wheel locations Side

Engine   Diesel

Originally built as the **Proud Lady** in 1977, the vessel was rebuilt after a fire in 1987 and renamed **Captain Proud** in 1989.

In 1993 the vessel entered the River Murray from the sea at the Murray mouth near Goolwa and travelled to Echuca. The **Captain Proud** has been located at Murray Bridge since 1995.

RIVER TALES

The First Steamboats

Time, isolation, floods, marshes and summer heat were all constant companions of the early explorers and settlers.

In dry seasons it was possible to walk from one side of the River Murray to the other. In times of flood the river was known to be up to 80 kilometres wide.

The opening up of the River Murray lead to many settlements along it. A major problem for the communities at these settlements was the moving of livestock, wool and other produce.

In 1852 in an effort to open up the river the Governor of South Australia, Sir Henry Young, offered a reward for the first steam boat to reach Swan Hill.

Two Paddlesteamers raced to Swan Hill in 1853. Francis Cadell's **Lady Augusta** and William Randell's **Mary Ann** reached Swan Hill within hours of each other, with the **Lady Augusta** taking the prize.

While the **Lady Augusta** was built in Sydney, the **Mary Ann** had the distinction of being the first Paddlesteamer built on the Murray and launched at Mannum in South Australia.

Murray Princess

Dimensions	67m x 15m x 1.5m
Built	1986 Goolwa
Paddle wheel location	Stern.
Engine	2 x 200hp Scania diesels.

The giant **Murray Princess** is the largest paddlewheeler built in the southern hemisphere, with three deck levels.

Offering trips of various lengths, The **Murray Princess** was purpose built for elegance and comfort, with spacious lounges and spiral staircases, while still providing disabled facilities. The tours take in Aboriginal culture together with natural and heritage sites.

PS Marion

Construction started on the **Marion** in 1896, including the building of its engine in Scotland. The death of the owner, George Fowler, in October of that year stopped the project. The trustees, in view of the cost of finishing the vessel, instructed that it be completed only as a barge. The barge Marion was launched at Milang in February 1897.

William Bowring purchased the barge in 1900 and by October that year it had been converted to a Paddle Steamer, carrying passengers and cargo.

In 1915 the **Marion** carried the Prime Minister, South Australia's Premier and other dignitaries along the lower Murray in celebrations to mark the building of the first lock. The NSW Premier stated that it was 'a journey for which no parallel can be found in Australia. I am sure it would be a highly popular trip if the attractions of it were better known.' That sentiment remains true today.

A fire in 1926 could have destroyed the **Marion** while it was tied up at Murray Bridge. At the time it was loaded with 500 cases of benzine, which caught alight after a flaming rag was accidentally dropped into the hold.

In 1963, after it had been used as a boarding house for several years, the **Marion** was purchased by the National Trust and the vessel went into dry dock at Mannum as a static museum. In 1989 a decision was taken to restore the boat to fully operational status, as this was the most practical way to preserve it.

On 1 November 1992 the then Governor of South Australia, Dame Roma Mitchell, officially refloated the **Marion**, with full restoration being completed in 1994.

PS Marion

Dimensions	33.5m x 6.9m x 1.6m
Built	1897 Milang
Paddle wheel locations	Side
Engine	wood fired steam

The **Marion** is now fully restored, with its wood fired engine, and is the only such original vessel offering overnight accommodation on a commercial ongoing basis.

The **Marion** is maintained and operated by volunteers, based only metres from the boiler of the **Mary Ann**, the first paddle steamer launched in the Murray.

Canally

Dimensions	18.7m x 4m x 1.5m
Built	1980, Berri by D. Wasley
Paddle wheel locations	Side
Hull	steel
Engine	IH 414 tractor

This new private pleasure vessel should not be confused with the original work boat **Canally** built in 1907, and sunk sometime before 1962.

Kingfisher

Dimensions	18.9m x 4.9m x 0.4m
Built	1989, Nathalia (near Echuca)
Paddle wheel locations	Side
Engine	Diesel

The original **PS Kingfisher**, a vessel of almost identical dimensions, was built near Moama in 1872, and broken up near Echuca in 1895 after a life of towing wool barges.

Photo	Michael Moseley

Tarella

Current location   7 kms above Mannum.

Dimensions   30.5m x 6.1m x 2.3m

Built   1897 Milang, composite hull

Paddle wheel locations   Side

The **PS Tarella** was built to carry 20 passengers, as well as for towing. In 1907 **Tarella** towed two barges to Goolwa with 1711 bales of wool, a massive cargo.

Tarella is now a stationary, privately owned houseboat, after having had several owners, including the South Australian Government.

RIVER TALES

The mythical bunyip lived in the River Murray and was the subject of many and varied tales, particularly for children.

At Murray Bridge it is possible to see a mechanical Bunyip which will rise from the water and roar for you. There is, however, another bunyip in the River Murray.

The **Bunyip** was a paddlesteamer built in 1858. In 1866 the **Bunyip**, while towing two barges, caught fire about 12 kilometres above Chowilla Station.

The fire rapidly took hold and all attempts to put it out were unsuccessful. Captain Randell decided to run the vessel into the bank in an attempt to save it and the 20 persons on board .

Unfortunately the steering jammed and the vessel circled helplessly in the middle of the river for sometime before eventually drifting on to one of the river banks when its engines stopped.

One woman passenger and her child died in the flames and two crew members also drowned while attempting to swim ashore. Most passengers and crew suffered burns.

The **Bunyip** was a total loss as were the barges it was towing. Captain Randell later managed to salvage one of the hulls and rebuilt it into the sailing vessel **Waterlilly**, which was also used on the River and lakes before it sank in Lake Alexandrina in 1903.

There is after all some basis of truth to the fables. There is at least one **Bunyip** in the River Murray.

Mayflower

Dimensions   14.5m x 3.9m x 1.1m, wood

Built   1884, Echuca

Paddle wheel locations   Side

Engine   converted from steam to diesel

First, and perhaps the most famous owner of the **Mayflower** was David Alexander, known as Black Alec. A West Indian Negro, he was reputed to have enormous strength and became somewhat of a legend on the River, and the subject of many bets amongst the River community.

Photo   Rod Morrison

Akuna Amphibious

Dimensions	23.4m x 4.9m x 1.7m
Built	1875, Melbourne
Paddle wheel locations	Side
Engine	Diesel

Renamed the **Akuna Amphibious** by its new owner in 1999 the former **Amphibious** featured in the films Gallipoli and The River Kings. The vessel was used as a showboat in the Port River, Adelaide for 12 years from 1959.

Akuna Amphibious is now at Akuna Station, between Kingston on Murray and Waikerie.

Photo	Sheri Schubert

PS Industry

Dimensions   33m x 5.6m x 2.6m

Built   1911, Goolwa

Paddle wheel locations Side

Engine   Steam

Industry was built for the South Australian Government as a work boat to clear the river bed. A new boiler was fitted in 1933 during an extensive refit.

Industry was moved to Renmark in 1970 for restoration and is now in use as a tourist vessel and floating museum.

Madam Jade

Dimensions	22.8m x 9m x 0.6m
Built	1991, Morgan
Paddle wheel locations	Side
Engine	Diesel

Madam Jade was built over four years as a home. Its owners travel the River selling bric a brac while living aboard the vessel.

The **Madam Jade** is the only trading riverboat on the Murray, recreating a tradition not seen for many decades.

Photographed at Renmark.

RIVER TALES

Customs

Pre Federation in 1901 each of the Australian States were separate colonies.

Crossing the River involved moving from one colony to another and resulted in customs duties being due for the movement of goods. This was also the case for moving cargo from one bank of the River Murray to the other.

Problems became common at low water if vessels had to be unloaded to allow them to draw less water. In theory a Customs Officer was needed to supervise the task. As the River was too shallow to navigate for approximately one third of the year this presented a significant problem.

Unloading a vessel following a breakdown would also draw the attention of Customs Officers.

For river boat captains it was not a simple case of navigating the River. Their responsibilities also took on the equivalent of moving from one country to another, more often associated with captains of ocean going vessels, not river boats.

The journey from Echuca - Moama to Goolwa involved passage through the separate colonies of New South Wales, Victoria and South Australia, each with its own Customs Officers and all alert for potential smugglers.

MILDURA

The Mildura Irrigation Colony, founded in 1887 by the Chaffey brothers, established Mildura as a city. The original Chaffey family home, **Rio Vista**, is today a museum.

The origin for this came when Alfred Deakin became a Member of the Victorian Parliament during a period of drought and recognised the importance of irrigation. During a trip to America in 1885 he met the Chaffey brothers, who came to Australia the following year.

Granted water pumping rights at Mildura, the region quickly developed, with a changed emphasis from wool to fruit production.

Delays in the importation and construction of pumps designed by the Chaffeys saw the use of the **PS Jane Eliza's** engine as the pump for this purpose at Psyche Bend, upstream from Mildura.

Mildura became a significant working river port for cargo and passengers. Today it is still the home of famous riverboats, but they carry tourists, not cargo.

Mildura is a centre of not only river activities but also wineries and many other tourist features including family theme parks. Although based on the River, Mildura is one of Australia's gateways to the outback.

A large well developed city, Mildura plays host to many special events, and is a major tourist destination.

Coonawarra

1950 saw the commissioning of a new riverboat, the Paddle Boat **Coonawarra**. Like many other riverboats, however, the **Coonawarra** started life as a barge.

Prior to 1950 and the addition of a superstructure and engine the **Coonawarra** was the barge **J L Roberts**. While the upper structure has only existed since 1950, her hull was built in 1884 and the paddle wheels came from the **PS Excelsior** with her shafts from the **PS Murrumbidgee**. In the post war environment material was short, and as well as parts from other vessels, significant other innovations were necessary to complete the **Coonawarra**, including the use of water pipes for hand rails.

In 1948 the **PS Murrumbidgee** was burnt and became a total loss. Its owners, Murray Valley Coaches Limited, had used her as a successful tourist passenger vessel and were anxious to replace her. The company had purchased the barge **J L Roberts** in 1946 together with the **Murrumbidgee** and decided that the barge, which was in good condition, would be used as the hull of a new vessel.

The **J L Roberts** had worked in the Echuca area carrying redgum from the Barmah Forests to the sawmills at Echuca, although it did spend significant periods out of the water when work was not available.

The new **Coonawarra** was designed by Charles Mackinnon, a naval architect, who took into account the ferries he had worked on as an apprentice on the Clyde. Many Echuca locals were critical of its features and believed her to be top heavy. This turned out not to be the case and full tests were carried out upon her which established her stability prior to her commissioning.

The **Coonawarra** has operated very successfully although at various times, like all riverboats, it was affected commercially by either floods or low water. It moved from Echuca interstate including a time at Murray Bridge before returning to Mildura where it now operates.

Coonawarra

Dimensions	34m x 6.8m x 2.6m, composite
Built	1884, Echuca as wool barge **J L Roberts**, rebuilt 1950 as passenger paddleboat
Paddle wheel locations	Side
Engine	diesel

The name **Coonawarra** is Aboriginal, meaning 'Black Swan'.

The paddlewheels of the **Coonawarra** came from the **Excelsior**, built at Goolwa in 1873

The **Coonawarra** sunk after hitting a snag in 1959. The vessel was quickly salvaged and repaired and today operates from the Mildura Wharf.

Avoca

Built at Milang in 1877 the **Avoca** remained on the River for 14 years.

In 1891 Darling and Co moved the vessel to Port Adelaide. The Avoca towed barges loaded with grain in South Australia's Gulf waters. In addition, as it was both self- propelled and shallow draughted it also carried grain from jetties to the huge sailing ships standing offshore in deeper water.

The ability of the **Avoca** to come into shallow water was of great benefit as it allowed grain to be easily loaded upon it from bullock drawn carriages. These carriages brought the grain to the water's edge, where **Avoca** was moored, enabling it to transfer cargo to larger ships anchored offshore in deep water.

Other riverboats, which were moved from fresh to salt water for service in South Australia's Gulfs, include the **Moorara** and **Ulonga**.

Sold in 1922, the Avoca again steamed through the Murray Mouth and began work in the River, operating as a tourist vessel out of Murray Bridge, after conversion from steam to diesel electric.

The Avoca moved to Mildura in 1976, where it is still used as a tourist vessel and floating restaurant. It remains one of the few vessels that have been in continuous operation, since its construction over 120 years ago.

Showboat Avoca

Dimensions   33.9m x 6.5m x 1.8m, iron

Built   1877, Milang

Paddle wheel locations   Side

In 1891 the **Avoca** was moved to Port Adelaide where it was used to tow barges around the Port River and South Australia's Gulfs, returning to the River about 1922.

Avoca was a popular cruise vessel at Murray Bridge for many years from 1957.

The **Avoca** is now a tourist vessel, operating as a showboat at Mildura since 1976.

Matilda

Dimensions	14m x 5.2m x 0.3m
Built	1997, Mildura
Paddle wheel locations	Side
Engine	Diesel

Matilda is a privately owned pleasure craft, operating in the Mildura region.

Impulse

Dimensions   21.9m x 5.2m x 1.5m

Built   1983-86, Colignan, above Mildura

Paddle wheel locations Side

Engine   Diesel

The **Impulse** is a privately owned pleasure vessel, and has cruised as far downstream as Goolwa. In 1988 Impulse participated in the Bicentennial Great Paddleboat Race at Goolwa, which was won by the **Rothbury**.

A barge of the same name was built in 1885 at Koondrook, and later abandoned at Moama.

Mosquito

Dimensions	10.7m x 3.5m x 1.1m
Built	1995, Colignan, above Mildura
Paddle wheel locations	Side
Engine	Diesel

Although one of the smallest paddleboats on the Murray, the **Mosquito** does not restrict its travels to its local area, travelling as far as Goolwa for the Wooden Boat Festival.

The original **PS Mosquito** was a slightly larger vessel built in 1857 at Dry Creek, north of Adelaide, and dragged by bullocks overland to be launched at Milang.

Kulkyne

Dimensions   18.3m x 4.9m x 0.3m

Built   1998, Mildura by Andrew Cook

Paddle wheel locations   Side

Engine   Diesel

The **Kulkyne** is a privately owned pleasure vessel, operating in the Mildura region of the River.

Photo   Peter Walmsley (owner)

Rothbury

Dimensions	26.8m x 6.1m x 0.9m, wood
Built	1881, Gunbower
Paddle wheel locations	Side
Engine	Diesel

Rothbury started her life as a timber barge towing vessel, although it was used for carriage of general cargo by various owners.

The **Rothbury** was used to tow barges until the 1950's and was converted to a tourist vessel over several years in the early 1970's, being changed over from steam to diesel during this period.

In 1896 the **Rothbury** narrowly lost a famous towing race against the **PS South Australia**, where each vessel was required to tow another paddlesteamer and two barges.

Photo   Lyn McKenzie

MV Loyalty

Dimensions   15.3m, Wood

Built   1914, Goolwa

Engine   Diesel

The **Loyalty** is a former milk boat which was used to carry dairy products to and from the factory at Murray Bridge. It also carried any other available cargo and passengers.

In addition to the **Loyalty**, the SA Farmers Union fleet included the **Co-operation**, **Progress** and **Union**.

The **Loyalty** now operates from Wentworth, at the junction of the Darling and Murray Rivers, with tours including Mildura.

PS Melbourne

Dimensions	29.9m x 6.4m x 0.9m composite hull
Built	1912, Koondrook
Paddle wheel locations	Side
Engine	wood fired steam

Melbourne was restored in 1965 and converted to a tourist vessel capable of carrying 300 passengers.

Melbourne was built as a snagging steamer, and for public works along the River when owned by the Victorian Government. It was fitted with a large winch for lifting fallen trees and snags, making it particularly useful assisting in the construction of bridges and weirs. Later towed timber barges.

Melbourne is one of the few vessels on the River still using her original steam engine.

Success

Dimensions   25.2m x 5.0m x 1.8m

Built   1877, Moama

Paddle wheel locations Side

The **Success** was used as a snagging vessel for a short time in the River Darling, with its main role being the towing of barges loaded with wool.

Success was used to rescue sheep from flooded stations during the 1956 floods.

Decades after being abandoned at Merbein, the **Success** was recovered and moved to the Old Mildura Homestead site in 1996 where its hull is currently undergoing restoration.

Photo   Frank Tucker

PS Mundoo

Dimensions	35m x 12m x 0.8m, steel hull
Built	1987, Hindmarsh Is, Goolwa
Paddle wheel locations	Side
Engine	Steam engine built in 1892, originally fitted to **Pyap**. Reconditioned and wood fired.

The **Mundoo** is a modern tourist vessel capable of carrying 200 passengers.

The original **Mundoo** was a 21m steam powered composite vessel, built in 1875 and was registered until 1938.

The **Mundoo** was moved from Goolwa to Mildura in 2000, by its new owners, where it operates in conjunction with the paddlesteamers **Melbourne** and **Rothbury**.

Shiralee

Dimensions	14.6 m x 4.0m x 0.3m
Built	2000, Mildura
Paddle wheel locations	Side
Engine	Diesel

The steel hulled **Shiralee** was launched in September 2000 for use as a private pleasure vessel.

Photo	Frank Tucker

RIVER TALES

Explosive Situations

Paddlesteamers needed to frequently stop and restock the wood for the fires of their boilers.

Professional wood cutters would chop wood and leave it stored at predetermined locations along the river bank. These stores were the historical equivalent of a fuel stop.

Vessels would restock during their trips, and as they pulled in to take on wood, they would sound their distinctive whistles or steam valves to let the wood cutters, who could be some distance away, know which vessel had taken the wood, for subsequent payment.

It was not unknown, however, for some boat owners wishing to avoid payment to cut their engines, drift quietly in to the bank, take on board the wood they needed, and drift silently off again.

The wood cutters in turn had their own means of retribution.

Explosives would be stuffed into hollow logs when certain boats were known to be in the vicinity. These special logs were then stored amongst the wood heaps.

Several boats suffered from unexpected explosions of their boilers. Rough justice, but effective.

SWAN HILL

A flock of noisy swans was responsible for the naming of Swan Hill in 1836.

Major Thomas Mitchell and his party were exploring the river system when the group was kept awake on the 21st June by these graceful, if somewhat noisy, birds leading him to record "I therefore named this isolated and remarkable feature Swan Hill".

Mitchell's reports of fertile soil and fresh water soon lead to the development of the area, and by 1847 a punt had been established across the River. Although the region was developed, the actual town of Swan Hill only had a white population of less than fifty almost eighteen years after its discovery.

The arrival of the first Paddlesteamers **Lady Augusta** and **Mary Ann** in 1853 quickly resulted in the development of Swan Hill as a riverport. Wool, grain and other produce were brought from the surrounding region for carriage downstream to Goolwa by boat, where it was onloaded to ocean going vessels.

Rail transport overtook the role of the paddlesteamers in 1890 for bulk cargo haulage and the riverboats predominantly carried passengers and general cargo for the next forty years.

Today Swan Hill is a modern city with a significant agricultural base. It is also well known for its Pioneer Settlement, which provides a view into life of yesteryear, with a remarkable reconstruction of an entire, fully operational, village. The **Pyap** runs daily cruises from within the Settlement, which is also the site of the **Gem** restoration.

PS Gem

Built at Moama in 1876, the **Gem** started her life as a barge. On her first trip she carried 200 tons of cargo to Hay while being towed by **PS Pearl**, returning with over 1,000 bales of wool.

The following year with the addition of an engine, paddlewheels and some accommodation facilities the **PS Gem** began operating as a general cargo boat.

Extended by over 12 metres in 1883 the **PS Gem**, was further totally refitted in 1939 specifically for the tourist trade and became so well regarded for her elegant fittings that she was known as the 'Queen of the Murray'.

The **Gem** sunk downstream from Mildura in 1948 when it took water after hitting a snag, but was refloated after 2 months.

In 1954 **PS Gem** made its last trip, from Morgan to Mildura. Eventually sold to Swan Hill the **Gem** was towed to Swan Hill in 1962 by the **Oscar W**.

The trip took far longer than expected as low water levels in the River resulted in both boats being stranded for six months at Goodnight.

The opening of the Swan Hill Pioneer Settlement as a major tourist attraction saw the role of the **Gem** change to a static museum. **Gem** is now undergoing full restoration.

PS Gem

Dimensions	40.7m x 6.2m x 2.0m
Built	1876, Moama
Paddle wheel locations	Side

Built as a barge, the **Gem** was fitted out as passenger steamer in 1877.

Gem was lengthened in 1883, by being cut in half at Goolwa and having 12.2m added amidships. After being cut in two, the halves were pulled apart by bullock teams.

Currently the Gem is undergoing restoration at the Pioneer Settlement in Swan Hill.

MV Kookaburra

Dimensions   25m x 7m

Built   1977, Port Adelaide

Engine   Diesel

The **Kookaburra** is licensed to carry 127 passengers, with cruises from Swan Hill to the famous Murray Downs Homestead.

A paddlesteamer of the same name was built at Goolwa in 1911. In 1952 during major flooding, the **PS Kookaburra** brought wool to Swan Hill, the first such visit for many years.

Pyap

Dimensions	28.7m x 5.1m x 1.2m
Built	1896 at Mannum
Paddle wheel locations	Side
Engine	Diesel

Built as a barge, **Pyap** had a steam engine fitted in 1898. A hawking steamer for 70 years, **Pyap** travelled 500kms each week as a floating shop while owned by Eudunda Farmers Co-op Stores of South Australia. **Pyap** was converted to diesel and used as a tourist vessel operating from Swan Hill Pioneer Settlement.

About 1970 **Pyap** was fitted out with a new steel hull for its use as a tour vessel. **Pyap** was burnt in 1978 but rebuilt.

Black Shag

Dimensions	16.0 m x 3.4 m x 0.4 m
Built	1999, Wallerawang, NSW
Paddle wheel locations	Side
Engine	Diesel

The **Black Shag** was launched at Swan Hill, after being built at Wallerawang. Reflecting a more modern era, **Black Shag** is of aluminium construction.

The privately owned boat has travelled about 3,000 kilometres between Swan Hill and Wellington.

Photo	Mick and Jean Turner (owners)

RIVER TALES

Locks and Weirs

The River Murray waters for millions of years have flowed directly into the sea, wasting precious fresh water in the driest Continent in the world.

Not only was it wasteful, but it caused major problems for the transportation of crops and cargo for the white settlers of Australia.

As well as the tyranny of distance, communities also faced the ever present problems of flood and drought.

The building of locks and weirs enabled the control of the River waters. The benefits were not only for navigation, but also for irrigation, enabling for the first time crops to be developed some distances away from the River at all times of the year.

The Barrages at Goolwa stopped sea water entering the Murray, and stopped the salinity problems experienced as far away from the mouth of the River as Murray Bridge.

The Hume and Yarrawonga weirs have no locks, creating a permanent barrier for boats into and out of the upper reaches of the River.

Elsewhere a system of locks enables the passage boats along the length of the Murray.

ECHUCA

Echuca on the Victorian side of the River, was once Australia's largest inland port.

About two hundred paddlesteamers working on the River used Echuca as their hub. Echuca's 1.2 kilometre wharf built in 1865 was a scene of activity second only to Melbourne. The huge red gum wharf has three levels, built to cope with the changing levels of the River.

Echuca is the closest River port to Melbourne and as such received the river trade from Queensland, New South Wales and Victoria for carriage by rail to and from Melbourne.

The opening of a rail link between Melbourne and Echuca in 1864 was a vital link and secured Echuca's prosperity. Ironically, the continued extension of the rail network also resulted in the demise of the river trade, and consequently many of the river towns.

The town was started by Henry Hopwood who ran a ferry service between Echuca and Moama on the New South Wales side of the River. An ex convict, Hopwood set up a series of floating barges which, with ropes and pulleys ferried people, livestock, wool and other produce from one side of the River to the other. It was an efficient, if expensive, service and made Hopwood a wealthy man.

The sheer volume of traffic is perhaps best illustrated by the fact that in its heyday Echuca boasted 79 hotels.

The region is also home to the world's largest redgum forests, and Echuca's boats and barges carried the giant logs felled by the thousands of workers who cut the trees and worked the sawmills.

Unlike in other parts of the world where logs were simply allowed to drift downstream, barges were necessary to carry the logs as redgum does not float. Logs were sunk in storage area in the River, and later lifted by grappling hooks onto barges.

Today the Port of Echuca has been restored to its former greatness, with particular emphasis on retaining its colonial heritage. It has the largest collection of paddlesteamers anywhere in the world, with even more paddlesteamers and paddleboats currently under restoration and construction.

Restored buildings and paddlesteamers attract large numbers of visitors who wish to capture the sights and sounds of yesteryear. The historic precinct of the Port of Echuca is based around the massive wharf, and includes displays and the opportunity to view **PS Hero** being restored.

Echuca is home to Australia's oldest paddlesteamer, **PS Adelaide**. It was also the location for the TV series 'All The Rivers Run', where **PS Pevensey** was temporarily renamed **Philadelphia**.

Paddle steamer cruises now operate many trips daily from the restored wharf area and nearby landings, and some also provide more extended trips.

Echuca itself is today a modern city with all facilities, developed in harmony with its historic past.

PS Adelaide

The Paddlesteamer **Adelaide** was built at Echuca in 1866.

Her maiden voyage was not without incident. The **Adelaide** crashed into the bank resulting in minor damage and injury to one person. The accident had been caused by a faulty reversing gear.

The **Adelaide** was a towing vessel and was not built with deck space for any significant amount of cargo. **Adelaide** would often tow two barges loaded with redgum logs from the Barmah Forest taking them to the sawmills at Echuca.

The **PS Adelaide** was sold in 1958 to the South Australian Sawmill Company and moved to Paringa.

In 1960 the Echuca Apex Club purchased the **PS Adelaide** and the vessel steamed back to to Echuca, where it was removed from the River and set in concrete as a display in Hopwood Park, adjoining the Wharf. It was not until 1982 that work commenced on the restoration of the hull, which eventually allowed the vessel to be recommissioned. In 1984, using heavy cable from across the River and two mobile cranes, the **Adelaide** was moved back to the water and moored at the Echuca Wharf.

Restoration work continued on her upper hull, deck and fixtures as well as the boiler. The **Adelaide** was recommissioned in 1985 by Prince Charles and Princess Diana.

The **PS Adelaide** is the oldest Paddlesteamer in Australia and the third oldest in the world. The Norwegian **Skibladner** was built in 1856 and the Danish **Hjejlen** in 1861.

PS Adelaide today operates as a tourist vessel from the Port of Echuca.

PS Adelaide

Dimensions	23.1m x 5.2m x 0.7m, wood
Built	1866, Echuca
Paddle wheel locations	Side
Engine	steam

Adelaide is Australia's oldest operating paddlesteamer.

Adelaide spent most of its life towing barges loaded with wood for the Echuca sawmills.

In 1963 it was removed from the water and set up as a display in Echuca's Hopwood Gardens. Refloated in 1984 after 4 years of restoration work, **Adelaide** was recommissioned in 1985.

PS Canberra

Dimensions   22.6m x 4.6m x 1.2m, wood

Built   1912, Goolwa

Paddle wheel locations   Side

Diesel was fitted in 1964, with the original steam engine being used for display purposes, although a reconversion to steam has been planned.

About 1960 **Canberra** was converted to a tourist vessel, after having been built as a fishing boat, then used as a cargo and pleasure craft.

Canberra has a 100 passenger capacity.

PS Pevensey

Dimensions	34m x 7m x 1.4m, composite.
Built	1910, Moama
Paddle wheel locations	Side
Engine	wood burning steam

The **Pevensey** is the largest vessel operating from Echuca wharf.

Pevensey sank in the late 1960's, but was refloated in 1968 and sold to Port of Echuca in 1973, where it was restored over three years.

Referred to by its owners as 'this giant Clydesdale of the River', it is able to carry 120 tons in its massive holds, and carry 90 passengers.

Temporarily renamed **Philadelphia** the vessel starred in the film 'All the Rivers Run', based on the book of the same name by Nancy Cato.

PS Etona

Dimensions	18.3m x 4.3m x 1.5m
Built	1898, Milang
Paddle wheel locations	Side
Engine	steam

The **Etona** was a mission boat until 1912 for the River Murray Church of England, prior to the construction of churches in riverside towns and communities.

In 1956 the **Etona** provided assistance to stranded stations when the Murrumbidgee flooded, with the river over eighty kilometres wide in places.

Restoration of the **Etona** began in 1962 after it was bought by Echuca residents.

In 1998 **Etona** visited South Australia for celebrations at Goolwa and Milang to mark the centenary of its construction.

PS Emmylou

Dimensions	30m x 10m, steel hull
Built	1982, Barham
Paddle wheel locations	Side.
Engine	Wood fired steam engine built 1906

The **Emmylou** was built with traditional appearance wooden topsides, and has cabins for 18 overnight passengers, with capacity for many more on regular day trips.

Emmylou is one of the few wood fired paddlesteamer cruise boats in the world offering overnight accommodation. **Emmylou** was named after American singer Emmylou Harris.

PS Alexander Arbuthnot

Built in 1923 at Koondrook, the Alexander Arbuthnot spent most of its early working life with Arbuthnot Saw Mills. The giant forests of the region provided extensive work for vessels, towing barges loaded with logs.

The barges were as large as the paddlesteamers that towed them, and were used to carry logs by having large cross beams placed across them with the heavy logs suspended beneath them.

The Alexander Arbuthnot sunk at Yeilima, about 120 kilometres above Echuca, in 1947 where it remained for over a quarter of a century. After being refloated in 1973 the Alexander Arbuthnot was taken to Shepparton for restoration.

In 1989 the vessel was bought by the Echuca Council. It was moved from Shepparton to Echuca in 1991 where its restoration was completed by the Port of Echuca.

The PS Alexander Arbuthnot now operates regular tourist trips from the Port of Echuca, where it is part of a growing fleet.

PS Alexander Arbuthnot

Dimensions   23.2m x 4.6m x 1.4m

Built   1923, Koondrook

Paddle wheel locations Side

Engine   steam

The **Alexander Arbuthnot** was built as a towing vessel for Arbuthnot saw mills. It sunk at Yeilima in 1947, was refloated in 1973, and taken to Shepparton.

The vessel was bought by the Port of Echuca in 1989 for tourist work, and was moved to Echuca in 1991 where its restoration was completed.

Alexander Arbuthnot has a capacity for 47 passengers.

PS Pride of the Murray

Dimensions   25.1m x 4.9m x 1.5m

Built   1924, Echuca as the timber logging barge C24.

Paddle wheel locations Side.

Engine   currently diesel

The **Pride of the Murray**, like many before her, started life as a barge, moving giant redgum logs.

At the end of its usefulness it was abandoned and sunk into the river bank where it filled with 250 tons of silt. In 1973, after significant difficulties, the silt was removed and the barge refloated and repaired at Moama slip. In 1977 it was converted for use as a tourist vessel.

The paddlewheels for **Pride of the Murray** came from **PS Hero**.

PS Perricoota

Dimensions	17.7m x 3.9m x 1.0m
Built	1999, Moama
Paddle wheel locations	Side
Engine	Steam

The new privately owned **Perricoota** is fitted with a Brown & May portable steam engine, built in 1909. Recycled materials have been used in the construction of its superstructure.

MV Mary Ann

Dimensions   20m x 8.2m x 1.2m

Built   1981, Goolwa

Engine   Twin diesel

The **Mary Ann** is a twin hulled cruise boat, specialising in functions and food service at Echuca.

The vessel moved to Echuca after time spent at Mannum, Goolwa and Berri as well as on the River Darling.

Captain Randell's original **Mary Ann** has made this a popular name, with at least seven vessels bearing the name.

Iron Dry

Dimensions	13.0 m x 3.2m x 0.4m
Built	1996, Wallerawang, NSW
Paddle wheel locations	Side
Engine	Diesel

The steel hulled **Iron Dry** was launched at Moama, after being built at Wallerawang. The privately owned boat has travelled about 7,000 kilometres between Tocumwal and Goolwa.

Photo   Mick and Jean Turner (owners)

PS Hero

Launched on 16 September 1874, the **Hero** was, according to contemporary newspaper accounts 'a pretty a little steamer as ever floated on the river' whose lines resemble those of a yacht more than anything else.

Hero had engines constructed either side of the central boiler, providing maximum power while taking up minimal space.

Hero was in use until 1957 when it burnt and sank at Boundary Bend, near Robinvale. Until its loss **Hero** towed barges, logs and carried other supplies, as well as being used as a hawking vessel on the Murrumbidgee River. **Hero** had been rescuing cattle stranded by floodwaters at the time it was burnt.

Over thirty years later the **Hero** was bought by Gary and Irene Byford, who removed the boiler and engine in 1991. It was to be a further seven years before the hull was raised after the removal of tones of mud and water, and moved to the Port of Echuca for restoration.

The re-launch of the hull occurred on 16 September 2000, the anniversary of its initial launch.

Photo provided by Port of Echuca

PS Hero

Dimensions	28.1 m x 5.2 m x 1.9 m
Built	1874, Echuca
Paddle wheel locations	Side
Engine	Original steam engines being refitted

The **Hero** was re-launched in September 2000, after restoration by the Port of Echuca. **Hero** is expected to be operational by mid 2001.

Originally used for towing barges for the sawmills, the **Hero** was burnt in 1957 at Boundary Bend. Purchased by its current owner in 1986, the **Hero** has been undergoing restoration since 1998 by the Port of Echuca's shipwrights. Its restoration marks a significant achievement, and adds to Echuca's status as the riverboat capital of the world.

Photo	Frank Tucker

PS Henry Charles

Dimensions	20.7m x 7.3m
Built	2000, Wyuna
Paddle wheel locations	Side
Engine	Steam, 10 hp Ruston Proctor, circa 1910

The steel hulled **Henry Charles** was built on a farm at Wyuna, then carried by semi trailer over 30 kilometres of road, and across the Echuca / Moama Bridge, to where it is now berthed below the Echuca wharf.

Photo	Jarrod Beer

The boats shown on this page from the Echuca area are typical of the many smaller privately owned vessels present on the River.

Sternwheeler PS Adventurous

Lady of Barmah

Killawarra
Photo: Matt Christopher

The tiny Gemma

James Maiden

75

RIVER TALES

Perils

Riverboats faced many and varied perils.

In times of drought boats could be stranded for many months if they were unlucky enough to be caught away from a deep part of the River. Commercially this was disastrous. At least one enterprising skipper caught in this situation used his engine to drive saw blades instead of paddle wheels, creating a temporary sawmill for the surrounding forest.

At the other extreme floods brought their own danger. Fast flowing waters made navigation difficult, particularly for the boats with lesser powered engines. The changing shape of the River during times of flood also raised the significant risk of boats hitting snags such as fallen logs, increasing the ever present risk of sinking. Rapidly receding flood waters could also leave the boat stranded large distances away from the River, as it was not unknown for the River to flood its banks by many kilometres.

Snags were a constant hazard to the riverboats, whose captains relied upon experience and hand drawn charts. Skippers of each boat were valued not simply for their ability to handle a vessel but also their navigation experience and knowledge of River hazards. Many boats on the River had their hull punctured by underwater snags, although fortunately most were able to be repaired or recovered.

Wood fired steam engines also created the ever present risk of fire aboard boats. Many vessels caught fire with several being total losses. The quickest and most effective way of quickly extinguishing a blaze was often to sink the vessel, enabling the later recovery of the remains and hopefully its cargo.

ALBURY

Albury is the furthest River port from the mouth of the Murray. Although Wodonga on the opposite side of the River was settled in 1835, the opening up of the Murray to navigation in the 1850's lead to the development of Albury.

Albury was a major producer of wheat and wool, but the volume and profitability of both was dependant upon rapid transportation. The distance between Albury and Adelaide was not a great problem once paddlesteamers were able to quickly move the produce.

The movement of cargo from Adelaide upstream to Albury also made return trips a sound financial proposition. Even though Adelaide was further than Melbourne and Sydney, it was more convenient due to its proximity and access to the River.

A wharf was constructed at Albury in the 1870's and catered to boats moving enormous quantities of wheat and wool.

The original **PS Cumberoona** was built at Echuca for the Albury Steam Navigation Company in 1866. Only seven years later, however, the railway reached Echuca and the days of the working paddlesteamer were numbered.

The current **PS Cumberoona** was built in Albury and launched in 1986 with support and funding from a Government Bicentennial Grant, Albury City Council, private and company sponsorship, a shipbuilding bounty and countless volunteers.

PS Cumberoona

Dimensions	25.2m x 6.5m x 1.0m
Built	1986, Albury
Paddle wheel locations	Side
Engines	2 wood fired steam built 1906 and 1908.

The **Cumberoona** was built with Bi-centennial funding, together with other grants and local fund raising. A unique feature are the two fully restored wood fired steam engines.

The **Cumberoona** is capable of carrying 136 passengers.

This vessel was named after the original **PS Cumberoona** built in 1866 and lost near Wilcannia 1889.

THE RIVERBOAT RENAISSANCE

The past 20 years or so have seen a major resurgence of interest in riverboats.

During this time many older boats have been restored to fully operational status, and wharf facilities repaired. The giant wharves at Echuca and Morgan are perhaps not the size as in their heyday, but the immense structures provide an insight to their past glory.

Australia's oldest paddlesteamer, **PS Adelaide**, is but one example of the new level of interest. After many years as a static land display, it now carries passengers from the Port of Echuca. Its historical value is made more significant when realising that it is the third oldest such operating vessel in the world. The two older vessels are in Scandinavia. For many years it appeared as if **Adelaide** would never be refloated, but a determined effort by countless enthusiasts has seen it fully restored, and carrying passengers.

For many years it was believed that the **PS Marion** would end its life as a museum display, resting on the river bed in its dock at Mannum. It is now fully operational and has recently celebrated its centenary. Its sister ships, **PS Gem** at Swan Hill and the **Ruby**, high and dry at Wentworth on the River Darling, are also undergoing restoration, although only the **Gem** is certain to be operational in the water again.

Historic boats such as the **Etona, Oscar W, Pevensey, Industry, Mayflower** and the former northern New South Wales tug **Leo** are typical of the benefits of such restoration work. All are wonderful and beautifully restored examples of older boats which previously plied the river. The Port of Echuca's **Alexander Arbuthnot** sunk at her moorings in 1947, was refloated in 1972 and subsequently restored.

Vessels such as the **Coonawarra, Melbourne, Avoca, Loyalty** and **Canberra** have been almost continually operational in one form or another,

79

and maintained diligently over recent years. The **Akuna Amphibious** has been fully renovated, and completely operational when sold recently as the **Amphibious**.

Historically many of the original paddlesteamers started their lives as barges, with their hulls being added to and converted to paddlesteamers, complete with engines and superstructure. Barges often had steering to help control them while being towed, so a conversion only required additional engine and paddle wheels, together with any necessary wooden cabins. It was not uncommon for decks and cabins to be altered during the life of a boat, as wood was an easy material to work with.

Amongst the most famous to be converted from barges were the **Marion, Coonawarra** and **Gem**. As the interest in paddlesteamers and riverboats has been rekindled in modern times this past tradition has continued. Echuca's **Pride Of The Murray** is a recent example of this. Derelict barges in or near the River may become the hulls of future boats, particularly with a growing value and respect for our river based heritage.

The interest in paddleboats has encouraged many new boats, including many featured within this book. A further ten and probably more .are currently being built or restored, including the **PS Hero** at Echuca.

The traditionally built **PS William Randell** at Goolwa, **PS Adventurous** and **PS Perricoota** at Echuca and the **Kulkyne** near Mildura are examples of modern riverboats, with the first three being powered by old restored steam engines.

The Bi-centennial project to build the twin steam engined **PS Cumberoona** at Albury is also indicative of the growing interest within the community to maintain links with our riverboat historical past.

Wooden boat and Steam festivals see many privately maintained and restored vessels present at the one location, often participating in events and carrying passengers. Some are only the size of rowboats with tiny steam engines. Others are full size boats. With every new event it is possible to really see the passion their owners have for riverboats. A passion shared by a growing number of visitors to the River.

THE RIVER MURRAY TODAY

The River Murray today is not simply a source of fresh water for the South East of Australia, but a major tourist region, with most towns and cities along its meandering length catering for visitors.

These men, women and children who visit the region from throughout Australia and overseas all have different expectations, both in terms of activities and facilities. The River does not disappoint, offering something for all.

Visitors include many who wish to enjoy riversports and also those using houseboats to travel the River enjoying its beauty, throughout their slow cruise. Most want to relax, in comfort varying from camping to luxury accommodation, either on land or water. Younger visitors often want activity and to be entertained. The River and its surrounds cater for all. A large number of national parks, together with extensive forests and lagoons provide an ever-changing vista for the visitor. The banks of the River are also home to much of Australia's natural wildlife and bird life. Both adults and children alike excitedly point to kangaroos, emus and parrots.

At the bottom of the River near Goolwa many varieties of ocean birds are seen, including large graceful pelicans. In this lower region the River is often separated from the ocean by no more than a few hundred metres of sand hills. Standing upon the barrages at Goolwa allows the visitor to see fresh water on one side and salt water on the other, when watching boats pass through the lock.

At the opposite end, in its upper regions above Albury-Wodonga, the River starts its flow beneath the Australian Alps where the flora and fauna reflect that environment, often mountainous and snow covered.

The River itself, of course, continues to provide pleasure for those who enjoy fishing. While no longer the home of significant numbers of the giant Murray cod, it still provides large catches of fresh water fish.

In addition to its attraction to tourists the River Murray is also Australia's principal wine producing area. While Australia has many famous wine growing regions, in South Australia, Victoria and New South Wales, more than 60 per cent of Australia's wine production is centred on the River Murray. The famous Canadian brothers William and George Chaffey introduced irrigation to the River's surrounding areas leading to major fruit production and extensive vineyards.

The Riverland is famous for its fruit and vegetables. Together with citrus, stone and dried fruit, nuts and wine grapes providing the basis for a major industry. Visitors have an abundance of attractions to visit, with many vineyards and orchards providing activities and facilities. Many wineries are attractions for visitors to the River giving wonderful opportunities to enjoy food and wine while at the same time appreciating magnificent scenery, ranging from tranquil lagoons to massive cliffs and sandy beaches. Major centres have a large variety of restaurants, hotels and other eateries, while even the smaller ones have family meals at the local hotels, which are often more community based than in large cities.

Commercial riverboats, both old and new, or hired modern houseboats provide an easy means for visitors to enjoy the River. The bustling elements decrease soon after leaving the towns, enabling visitors to enjoy the tranquillity the River has to offer.

Benefits from irrigation are clearly seen as visitors travel to the River often passing major stretches of desert and in some cases bare plains. It is only necessary to be a few kilometres from the River itself to be in some of the driest land Australia has to offer. The irrigated areas are like an oasis, full of life and colour.

In the past the River was a vital means of trade and transport, with boats and barges each carrying hundreds of tons of cargo. Today, with modern road and rail transport, it no longer serves this purpose, but continues to see many boats travelling upon it carrying tourists rather than cargoes of wool, grain and general supplies. With the increasing number of riverboats we now see tens of thousands of visitors enjoying trips from each of the ports.

The length of the River and its easy accessibility for most of Australia's population has made it an important tourist destination. Townships and communities along its length have now grown to major proportions by Australian standards, and in many cases are no longer dependent upon the River as the sole means of their survival, although its importance is unquestioned. The Murray-Darling basin contains 42% of all Australian farms, with over half of Australia's orchards along the River. Cattle and dairy industries continue to be significant, together with the production of wool, wheat, cotton, rice and oil seed.

Tourism plays a major role in River activities with industries centred around visitors destinations.

Apart from scenic beauty and extensive range of food and wine, purpose built tourist attractions are to be found. Catering to both family groups and individuals more interested in historical or special interest sites. The redevelopment of port facilities and the restoration of many old paddlesteamers provide an opportunity for visitors to experience even short trips along the River in these magnificent boats.

Major port facilities exist at Goolwa, Mildura, Swan Hill and Echuca with the central feature being the town wharves and related activities. Visiting to these locations allows guests to undertake cruises ranging from an hour or two to more extended periods of up to a week. In addition, all offer a wide range of other attractions, making them significant tourist destinations. At Goolwa these tours include the world famous Coorong as well as the River itself.

Beyond the more established larger ports, Mannum, Murray Bridge, Renmark and Albury provide commercially operated boat trips, although some of these do not operate every day. Many other commercial or privately owned boats are also found at various points along the River. They range in size from canoes to modern cruise boats capable of carrying well over one hundred passengers.

The River today continues to be a place of beauty, offering hospitality and facilities to its residents and visitors alike.

RIVER MANAGEMENT

The water catchment area of the Murray, Darling, Lachlan and Murrumbidgee Rivers covers nearly one eight of the continent, and passes through several states.

The River Murray Commission established in 1917 regulates the sharing of water between the States of New South Wales, Victoria and South Australia, for the benefit and security of all.

Each State continues to have its own water authority responsible for the construction of locks and weirs under the co-ordination of the Commission.

The Murray-Darling Basin Commission superseded the earlier body in 1988.

Originally set up to manage water levels to assist river traffic, the Commission's role changed with the demise of the riverboat trade to a focus upon irrigation.

In more modern times its role includes environmental and water quality management to ensure sustainability of this invaluable natural resource.

EARLY ABORIGINAL LIFE

The River Murray basin was formed millions of years ago, with the River as we know it today forming approximately two hundred thousand years ago.

The abundant fresh water meant that wild life was attracted to the area and the River became a home to a large variety of animals and bird life.

Fifty thousand years ago saw the arrival of Aboriginal people. The ready availability of fresh drinking water together with fish, animals and bird life provided an ideal environment for them to live.

This time also saw the stabilisation of climatic conditions. The effect of this was that the riverland and its flora and fauna started to take on the appearance that we are familiar with today. The River had extensive fish life and attracted large numbers of waterfowl and other bird life, as well as kangaroos.

The Aboriginal people lived along the Murray in large numbers for almost 50 thousand years, with abundant supplies of food and water together with the necessary materials for shelter and other living requirements.

Today, traditional Aboriginal life is seen by the world in desert images, against a backdrop of ochre coloured sand and rock. The only water in such images being the occasional billabong, but overwhelmingly the heat and dryness of the surroundings are the dominant features.

In the past, the situation was very different. Almost 100 different tribes formed separate communities along the River, the riverland region and south eastern Australia, in what today are the fertile regions of New South Wales, Victoria and South Australia.

Similarly to today, the majority of Australia's pre-colonial population occupied the south east portion of the continent.

The Aborigines living along the River developed quite different skills from the communities living in the drier parts of Australia. The development of canoes, made from the bark of river gums, enabled the easy movement along the River and also provided the means for fishing. Nets were also used as well as spears and the environment they lived in dramatically shaped their way of living. Freshwater mussels contributed significantly to the staple diet, with large mounds of shells today remaining as evidence not only of what was eaten, but also of the fact that the riverland Aboriginals were not nomadic.

It was a very different lifestyle from that of the Aboriginal communities living in the rest of Australia, who constantly moved to find food and water.

This traditional lifestyle continued until the mid-1800's, when the arrival of European settlers had a dramatic impact. The taking over of the riverland by white settlers for farming and grazing displaced the land's original owners, and the introduction of European diseases decimated the Aboriginal population. The lack of immunity to such diseases as measles and smallpox all but wiped out entire tribes.

The survival of Aboriginal communities in the more arid regions of Australia owed much to the fact that Europeans at that time were only interested in areas that they could farm, with ready access to fresh water, and to safe harbours. The most effective protection for Aboriginal life and culture at the time was isolation and lack of contact with Europeans.

For a race that survived over 50,000 years, the past 200 years have been the most traumatic, with dramatic cultural changes in the space of six or seven generations.

Today, many descendants of the original tribes still live along the River, generally as part of local communities made up of varying cultural and ethnic backgrounds. Their history is often reflected in place names, such as

Echuca, derived from the Aboriginal language meaning "the meeting of the waters". The famous Coorong, the narrow stretch of water at the Murray Mouth, is named after the Aboriginal word for neck, "Kurangh".

Swan Hill was named after the swans that kept early explorers awake, but these same swans gave their name to the graceful riverboat Coonawarra, the Aboriginal word meaning black swan.

THE HAWKING STEAMERS

The hawking steamers, or floating stores, were absolutely vital to the communities living along the River. The **Pyap**, currently at the Swan Hill Pioneer Settlement, started its life as such a floating store. Others were the **Prince Alfred**, **Queen**, **Marion**, **Saddler**, **Emily Jane**, **Merle** and **Kookaburra**.

The **Hero**, recently relaunched at Echuca after years of restoration, was also employed in this way on the Murrumbidgee River.

Australia's first paddlesteamer built and launched on the River Murray, the **Mary Ann**, sold flour and groceries to settlers along the riverbank as it travelled upstream on its historic trip in 1853.

Today the only such vessel on the River is the recently built **Madam Jade**.

A significant problem for these hawking vessels pre federation was intercolonial movement. Crossing from one side of the River to the other required Customs clearance and tax payments before any goods could be landed or sold. The River Murray paddlesteamer trade existed because of the relatively swift transport available by water. Although the majority of vessels carried bulk cargo such as wool and grain, or else towed barges laden with logs for the sawmills, the hawking boats also thrived because they met a vital community need. Trips, which could take weeks overland, could often be undertaken in days by boat.

The hawking boats not only serviced existing communities along the River, but their very existence made it possible for many settlers to move to the River and establish farms and homes.

Boat owners who made their living carrying cargo for stores in the major towns generally did not operate these hawking vessels, as they did not want to compete with their main customers. They were bulk cargo carriers rather than storekeepers.

Sufficient work existed, however, for boat owners whose main business was not freight haulage, to provide a vital service for those many people living along the River away from major towns.

In an era where transport was often difficult and slow the hawking boats provided both social contact and ready access to the many settlers along the River.

They were particularly important to the women living along the River whose ability to leave their homes or farms was greatly limited. Theirs was often an isolated existence, more often than not restricted by lack of transport and the need to stay with children. They were unable to travel regularly to nearby towns, except for special occasions. The floating stores did much to break the isolation, providing essential supplies and social contact.

These vessels carried everything, ranging from machinery and farm equipment right through to food supplies and clothing. The speed of transport also meant that it was possible to supply fresh food to remote settlers, who without these boats had to rely on supplies of salted or otherwise preserved alternatives.

Today mobility and communication is taken for granted with good roads, fast communication, and ready access to telephones, television and other associated comforts. In the heyday of these hawking steamers such luxuries did not exist and the role they played was significant. Even homesteads located as close as 20 kilometres from major centres were in effect isolated by the poor roads and lack of general transport.

The development of roads and private cars together with rail transport spelled the death of the hawking steamers that played such an important role in the development of this part of Australia.

The **Madam Jade**, the only hawking vessel operating today, exists because its owners have chosen this lifestyle. It attracts attention whenever and wherever it ties up to welcome customers aboard.

Unlike the essential supplies carried by earlier trading boats, the **Madam Jade** sells old wares, collectables, bric-a-brac, gifts, toys and souvenirs.

MILK BOATS

Murray Bridge, 110 kilometres from the Murray Mouth, was the site of a dairy produce factory in the early 1900's, receiving milk and cream from dairies in the region and producing butter and other products.

The collection of milk from dairy farms along the River was better suited to smaller motor vessels, generally about 12 to 15 metres in length, than the larger and more cumbersome paddlesteamers.

These smaller vessels called into the dairies, delivered groceries, mail, smaller cargo and sometimes passengers approximately 20 kilometres either side of Murray Bridge, and collected milk for delivery daily to the factory.

Many smaller boats were used in this industry, with SA Farmers Union owning its own fleet, comprised of **Co-operation**, **Loyalty**, **Progress** and **Union**. Two of these vessels are operational today with the **Loyalty** based at Wentworth and the **Progress** privately owned at Goolwa. A third, the **Union** is undergoing restoration at Murray Bridge.

The boats were capable of being handled by one person, which in view of their daily schedule, made them both convenient and economical to run. This was an important consideration as the paddlesteamers required a crew to operate them and were incapable of operating in amongst the many creeks flowing into the River.

Most boats carried out two runs daily, the first before dawn and the other around noon. The runs took place seven days a week, irrespective of season or weather.

The boats were fully covered to provide shade for the cans of milk, but were not enclosed on the sides, enabling the cans to be conveniently loaded along their length from the little jetties at each dairy. Often these jetties were no more than rickety planks amongst the reeds, strung across poles which were pushed into the shallow waters out from the riverbank.

A JOURNEY IN TIME

Two hundred thousand years ago the River Murray basin as we now know it was formed. Fifty thousand years ago saw the arrival of people to the area, with Aboriginals arriving from countries to the North of Australia.

The Aboriginal communities along the River lived, fished and hunted undisturbed until the arrival of white settlers in the early 1800's.

Captain Charles Sturt explored the River system in 1830 using a whaleboat and established that the Murrumbidgee River flowed into the Murray and that its Mouth was in the vicinity of Goolwa.

Settlers quickly moved to occupy the land along the River but soon found that the tyranny of distance made it difficult to move large amounts of wool and grain long distances overland.

Goolwa was quickly established as a riverport of major significance, providing ready access to ocean crossing sailing ships. Cargo could be

moved on boats through the Murray Mouth, or overland a short distance to Port Elliot and to a lesser extent Victor Harbour.

Punts, or ferries, across the River were the predecessors of the many bridges of today. They were often the sites of towns which grew up either side of the River, each in a different colony in the case of Victoria and New South Wales.

Today, although seen by many as one town or city, locations such as Echuca-Moama and Albury-Wodonga reflect the independent development that took place on opposite banks of the River.

The River formed a perfect highway for the carriage of goods, and in 1853, in answer to the demands for rapid transportation the Paddlesteamers **Lady Augusta** and **Mary Ann** were the first to travel from the lower Murray to Swan Hill. This marked the beginning of the Riverboat era, which saw paddlesteamers and riverboats used to move cargo and passengers relatively quickly across vast distances.

The founding of the Mildura Irrigation Colony in 1887 saw the start of water management, with the Chaffey brothers managing 250,000 acres of land. An Irrigation Trust subsequently took over responsibility for water distribution.

Prior to Federation movement across the Murray involved crossing from one colony to another, each with its own Customs requirements. Federation played an important role for the whole of Australia but had particular significance to those communities living near or relying on the River.

Federation in 1901 allowed, for the first time, goods to be moved freely along the River without concern for State borders. It also saw the start of national programs which managed the flow of water, both for irrigation and navigation.

The difficulties caused by changing river levels during floods or drought resulted in the construction of 26 locks and weirs between 1915 and 1940. These barriers provided a means of regulating water flow, enabling the River to be navigable at all times.

These control barriers have also created some problems for South Australia at the lower end of the flow of the River Murray, as Governments controlling the upper reaches exercise control over the quality and quantity of water released downstream. This continues as a problem to the present day.

The river trade saw the development of a significant number of large towns and major centres such as Goolwa, Echuca, Swan Hill, Morgan and Mildura together with many smaller riverports.

Wharves at Echuca, Mildura, Morgan and Goolwa were the sites of large numbers of boats, often tied several deep, side by side, along the length of each wharf, and well beyond.

These massive structures, particularly at Echuca and Morgan, were not only very long, but several stories high, to provide access for the boats whatever the water level of the River.

The changing face of the riverboat trade saw vessels initially used for hauling large quantities of wool and grain continue until the turn of the century when rail transport became faster and more economical.

The introduction of rail saw another phase in the River's development, with the building of railheads and populations of towns growing to cope with the construction and ongoing operation of railways.

For thirty or more years after rail was introduced many of the riverboats continued to be viable as passenger vessels. Their numbers have dramatically reduced until today when the major role for paddlesteamers and riverboats is the tourist trade. The romance of paddlesteamers has lead to many of the boats now being restored and many new boats being constructed.

One hundred years after Federation sees in the order of fifty operational paddlesteamers and riverboats upon the River. Although a far cry from their heyday this still represents a significant reminder of our River heritage.

EARLY NAVIGATION

Early navigation of the River Murray was difficult. Not only did riverboat captains have to face the changes brought about by flood or drought, but had to do this without maps.

During times of flood, the River was often many kilometres wide, making the main channel hard to find, as well as the added danger brought about by floating trees or submerged logs and debris. The speed of the current flow added to the danger, particularly when towing barges.

Drought brought its own problems, with low water creating new hazards from sand bars and reefs. Until the building of locks the River was unnavigable for up to four months of each year. The River did not present a constant face.

A captain's knowledge of these hazards was vital, and each had his own personal hand drawn charts. These scroll like charts, about 40cms wide and several metres long, were hand wound from one roll to the other, and included all the information that a captain could gather. Details of rock locations during times of low water, for example, could make the difference between a successful journey and disaster.

Unlike today when commercial charts are available to all, these hand drawn charts were the property of individuals, and were an item of great value. The charts were continually updated by their owners, as their accuracy gave them a competitive edge in the river trade.

It was not just a captain's skill that produced a successful journey, but the accuracy of their charts.

RIVERBOATS

The development of Australian riverboats was quite unique, taking into account local circumstances.

Riverboats used by Aboriginal communities living along the river system were bark canoes cut from the giant river gums. These canoes generally carried individuals, although they were capable of carrying more than one person in the right conditions.

The coming of white settlers led to the rapid development of European Communities along the River, and brought about the need to move large amounts of cargo quickly. Initially this was carried out using boats with oars, such as whaleboats, or small sailing vessels but these were unsuitable for commercial use.

The South Australian Government, in an effort to encourage the development of a river trade, offered a reward in June 1850 to the first steamboat to travel upstream to the River Darling junction.

Captain William Randell built the PS MARY ANN at Mannum, and in 1853 was ready to undertake the trip. The 16.8 metre long vessel was first taken downstream to Goolwa to obtain Customs clearance before proceeding back upstream, and into the waters of the colonies of Victoria and New South Wales.

At the same time Captain Francis Cadell put a proposal to the South Australian Government for a payment of 2,500 pounds if he was to bring a paddlesteamer into the Murray, and to take it and a barge to the junction of the River Darling, and to continue to operate it in the River for a year.

The offer was accepted and the 30.2 metre **Lady Augusta** entered the River through its mouth and took the Goolwa built barge **Eureka** in tow.

The **Lady Augusta** reached Swan Hill only hours ahead of the **Mary Ann** on 17 September 1853. Captain Randell received 300 pounds, although he subsequently received a further 400 pounds from public subscription.

Since the first use of paddlesteamers in the River Murray in 1853, their development reflected the needs of the settlers. Riverboats were used for varying functions and were designed accordingly.

Unlike the giant American sternwheelers, Australia's river system and the River Murray in particular made it necessary for a different design. The often narrow, and always twisting, nature of the River led to the predominant design for paddlesteamers being side wheeled rather than stern driven.

The use of side wheels enabled these vessels to more easily negotiate the many bends found along the River. Such mobility would not have been possible with stern propulsion, as in most cases the stern wheel would strike the bank as the boat negotiated bends. The Mississippi style sternwheelers were also not practical for towing, as the barges could strike and damage the wheel.

A limited number of sternwheelers were built, such as the **Captain Sturt**, which was used to push rock-laden barges during the construction of the locks.

Vessels served different purposes and their designs varied accordingly.

The first paddlesteamers were used to move large amounts of wool, and while boats themselves could carry some cargo, this was generally undertaken by towing barges behind them.

Barges could be loaded with up to 2000 bales of wool, enabling huge quantities to be moved quickly. A master was responsible for steering the barge while under tow, and did this with a temporary wheel fixed on top of the cargo, with chains running back to the rudder.

The barges themselves were often as large as the vessels that towed them, and in fact barges were often converted to paddlesteamers with the addition of a steam engine and superstructure.

The other main use of these boats, particularly in the upper regions of the Murray, was to haul enormous quantities of timber logs.

Trees were felled in the giant red gum forests and dragged to the river where they were slung either side of barges and towed to the many sawmills operating along the River. Echuca was a main centre for such activity.

Australia's oldest operational paddlesteamer, **Adelaide**, was such a log barge towing boat, as was the **Alexander Arbuthnot**. The **PS Pride of the Murray** started its life as the timber logging barge C24.

Barges were used not only for carrying felled tree trunks, but also the processed timber after it had been cut to size at the sawmills.

Smaller vessels were used for fishing where speed and power was not as critical. These smaller vessels were also used to move smaller amounts of cargo between riverports. The 14.5 metre **Mayflower**, built at Echuca in 1884, was used for this purpose, as well as being a trading boat. The 1912 built **Canberra** also started its life as a fishing boat.

Religion was often not far from people's minds and needs, and another more unusual role for some smaller vessels was as mission boats or floating churches. These boats, such as the **Etona** and **Glad Tidings**, regularly visited the many communities and isolated properties along the River, performing all of the roles traditionally associated with churches.

In 1998, to mark the centenary of its construction, the **Etona** returned to Milang, where many gathered in period costume to celebrate the event. The highlight for many was the conduct of a marriage at the end of the Milang jetty, where **Etona** and several other paddlesteamers and riverboats were tied.

As the population increased and the number of towns along the River grew, passenger vessels became more popular. These boats were generally much larger than their workhorse counterparts and often had several decks with passenger accommodation. They were often quite elegant, a far cry from the barge towing boats used for heavy haulage of either the wool or timber. The **Marion** and **Gem** were two of the better known passenger vessels. Smaller propeller driven vessels were also used where maneuverability and ease of handling were critical, such as the milk boats calling in to dairies along the River.

Today we see a variety of riverboats ranging from restored original paddlesteamers through to large modern cruise vessels carrying tourists. Echuca, Mildura, Goolwa, Swan Hill, Mannum, Murray Bridge, Albury and Renmark have commercially operated boats, many of which are historic.

Many of these vessels, and their privately owned counterparts, will travel downstream to Goolwa in late 2001 to mark the centenary of Federation, in what will be the largest gathering of paddlesteamers and riverboats seen together in modern times.

In addition, technology has now developed to the point where many smaller, and sometimes faster vessels, are used to provide visitors with ready access to the River. Houseboats are growing in number, with many thousands of people hiring these for holidays along the River, enabling their occupants to travel the waters that once could only be seen from paddlesteamers.

These modern boats may not be as romantic as traditional old paddlesteamers, but serve an important role by allowing many to enjoy ready access to the River.

EARLY DAYS

BIBLIOGRAPHY

$\mathbf{M}$uch of the research in this book has come from secondary sources. The author gratefully acknowledges the valuable information from the following books and publications, all of which are highly recommended to readers interested in this fascinating subject.

Baker. R & M, Reschke. W . . . .*Murray River Pilot*

Bevan. G & Vaughan. M . . . .*Mannum Yesterday*

Godson. H . . . .*The Marion Story*

Lawson. W . . . .*Paddle-Wheels Away*

Loney. J . . . .*Wrecks along the Murray*

McNicol. S . . . .*Murray Paddleship Review*

Mudie. I . . . .*Riverboats*

Painter. G . . . .*In the wake of the Coonawarra*

Parsons. R . . . .*Paddle Steamers of Australasia*

Parsons. R . . . .*Ships of the Inland Rivers*

Phillips. P . . . .*Riverboat Ways*

Wasley. D (ed) . . . .*Australian Steam Power Journal*

Williams. R . . . .*River Murray Journal*

Williams. R . . . .*The Paddle Steamer Marion*

INDEX OF BOATS

ACKNOWLEDGMENTS

Riverboat people have a passion for their boats. Any inquiry was enthusiastically responded to, often with more information about other boats.

In all cases people went out of their way to be helpful. This included boat builders, owners, crews and the countless volunteers associated with restoration work.

I only wish that this book was double its size to be able to include more of the information gathered.

Thank you in particular to those who supplied information and photos. Photos not taken by me have been acknowledged within the book.

Thanks also to people who have provided advice and photos which for space reasons could not be used within this book.

Particular thanks also to my wife Joy and son Matt who have provided advice and support, as well as enduring countless trips as I gathered information and took hundreds of photos.

Peter Christopher

ABOUT THE AUTHOR

P eter Christopher has had a keen interest in maritime history, and has been diving on shipwrecks, for over 30 years.

Peter has dived on wrecks throughout Australia, and also on historical sites in the River Murray. It was during more recent dive trips he developed an interest in riverboats.

Peter's voluntary contribution to the field of maritime archaeology received national recognition in the form of an Award presented to him by the Commonwealth Government in 1982.

He is still active in research and diving activities, and is constantly upgrading an extensive computer data base of shipwreck and maritime information which he established. Peter is the author of four other books, including the highly valued reference work 'South Australian Shipwrecks. A Data Base. 1802-1989'.

Peter Christopher lives in Adelaide. He is often to be found cruising the waters of the lower Murray around Goolwa and the Coorong.

Photo: Kym Winter-Dewhirst